THE BIG BOOK OF SHARKS

SHARK WEEK
25 JAWSOME YEARS

TIME HOME ENTERTAINMENT
Publisher Richard Fraiman
Vice President, Business Development & Strategy Steven Sandonato
Executive Director, Marketing Services Carol Pittard
Executive Director, Retail & Special Sales Tom Mifsud
Editorial Director Stephen Koepp
Editorial Operations Director Michael Q. Bullerdick
Executive Publishing Director Joy Butts
Director, Bookazine Development & Marketing Laura Adam
Finance Director Glenn Buonocore
Associate Publishing Director Megan Pearlman
Assistant General Counsel Helen Wan
Assistant Director, Special Sales Ilene Schreider
Design & Prepress Manager Anne-Michelle Gallero
Brand Manager Katie McHugh
Associate Prepress Manager Alex Voznesenskiy
Associate Production Manager Kimberly Marshall

SPECIAL THANKS TO Andy Dehart, Christine Austin, Jeremy Biloon, Stephanie Braga, Jim Childs, Susan Chodakiewicz, Rose Cirrincione, Lauren Hall Clark, Jacqueline Fitzgerald, Christine Font, Jenna Goldberg, Hillary Hirsch, Suzanne Janso, Mona Li, Amy Mangus, Robert Marasco, Amy Migliaccio, Nina Mistry, Dave Rozzelle, Adriana Tierno, Vanessa Wu

ISBN 10: 1-60320-930-1
ISBN 13: 978-1-60320-930-4

Published by Time Home Entertainment Inc.
135 West 50th Street • New York, NY 10020

Produced by Downtown Bookworks Inc.
Written by Jack Silbert
Designed by Charles Kreloff
Editorial Assistant: Sara DiSalvo
Special thanks: Sarah Parvis, Patty Brown, Nathanael Katz, Kal Katz, Maccabee Katz

Discovery CHANNEL

THE BIG BOOK OF SHARKS

SHARK WEEK
25 JAWSOME YEARS

ABOUT
SHARK STATS

**Throughout the book, the length
and weight listed in Shark Stats
refers to the shark's *average*
size. In the text, you may see
mention of a particular species'**

CONTENTS

THE DEADLIE

When a lemon shark, blue shark, or hammerhead patrols the waters, pray you aren't the prey. Of course, most sharks aren't deadly. Out of more than 400 shark species in the world's oceans, fewer than 10 percent have ever attacked a human. But the stats aren't much comfort when those powerful jaws clamp shut—serrated teeth digging into flesh—and the thrashing begins.

Sharks are meat-eaters, consuming about 5 to 10 percent of their body weight every week. Sharks chow down on a lot of fish, squid, dolphins, sea lions, and even other sharks. Humans aren't on the menu, but can sometimes be mistaken for prey.

Let's get a closer look at the top 10 sharks you wouldn't want to run into.

Lemon shark

THE DEADLIEST SHARKS
LEMON SHA

SHARK BITE *Its scientific name,* Negaprion brevirostris, *comes from the words for "smooth teeth" and "short snout."*

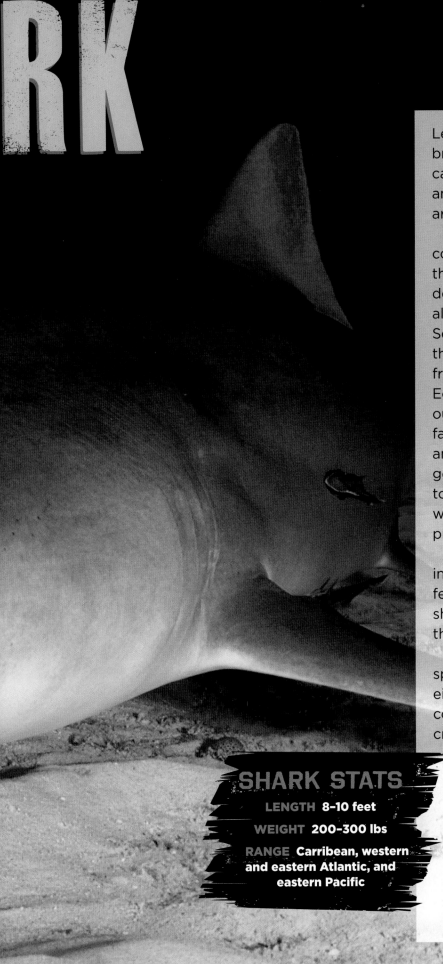

Lemon sharks have a yellowish-brown coloring that is great camouflage above the sandy and muddy bottoms where they are often found.

The lemon shark is found in coastal waters. In the Atlantic, they live from New Jersey down to southern Brazil, and also on the African coast along Senegal and the Ivory Coast. In the Pacific, they can be found from Baja, California, down to Ecuador. Though they hang out in the same coastal waters favored by swimmers, divers, and surfers, lemon sharks are generally not a great threat to humans. However, they will respond vigorously when provoked.

Social sharks, they gather in small schools at night to feed, often near fishing piers in shallow water. In the daytime they retreat to deeper spots.

Lemons are a larger shark species, usually in the range of eight to 10 feet long. Their diet consists mainly of bony fish and crustaceans.

Mating takes place during the spring in shallow water. Females are pregnant for 10 to 12 months. They return to shallow water and give birth to anywhere between four and 17 live pups. These young sharks stay put for several years.

SHARK STATS

LENGTH 8-10 feet

WEIGHT 200-300 lbs

RANGE Carribean, western and eastern Atlantic, and eastern Pacific

You're shipwrecked—the only survivor. Struggling to stay afloat in the wide open ocean. Then you notice something...it's circling you...and circling...and circling....

The blue shark isn't particularly aggressive, but it won't pass up a chance for a meal. For 15 minutes or more, one might circle a diver or swimmer before moving in for a sample bite.

Their normal diet consists of a variety of fish, squid, and maybe the occasional seal. (Sometimes it's kill or be killed: the sea lion can also be a predator of the blue shark.) Again, not one to ignore a ready meal, the blue shark will snag food out of fishermen's nets and from fishing lines. Of course, sometimes the shark then gets caught up in these same nets and lines.

The blue is a large shark, growing to lengths of 13 feet and weighing up to 450 pounds. It can be found in all of the world's oceans, as far north as Norway and as far south as Chile. The shark is happiest in water temperatures ranging from 45 to 60 degrees Fahrenheit. Generally, they're not found near shore. In tropical waters, blue sharks are found at greater depths, where the water is cooler. In temperate waters, the blue shark is closer to the surface.

Even so, they might not be easily spotted. The appropriately named shark is dark blue on top, bright blue on the sides, and white underneath. The coloring provides camouflage in the ocean.

SHARK BITE *Certain parasites love the blue shark. Up to 3,000 might live on the shark at a time, on its pectoral fins, in the nose, on the skin, and in the gills.*

SHARK STATS

LENGTH 7–13 feet

WEIGHT 300–400 lbs

RANGE Cold water, in oceans around the world

BLUE SHARK

The blue shark's pointy, serrated teeth make it easier to catch slippery squid (its favorite meal)!

HAMMERHE

It's easy enough to spot a hammerhead shark—it's the one with a flat, hammer-shaped head. But first, you might spot the tall fin sticking out of the water. Of course, you might not know which hammerhead you're looking at: There are nine or possibly 10 different species. They range from three feet long up to 20 feet, and the biggest ones can weigh as much as 1,000 pounds. Hammerheads are found in temperate and tropical coastal waters worldwide, though they tend to migrate to cooler water in the summer.

Larger hammerheads are potentially dangerous to humans. They certainly have a diverse appetite, eating everything from invertebrates to other sharks. Though many hammerheads form schools during the day, they hunt alone by night. And they are particularly good at finding prey. With eyes at the ends of their flat faces, hammerheads have a wide range of vision. And with sensory organs spread out across that wide face, it's even easier to locate sources of food. Their favorite meal: stingrays.

When it's time to mate, males like big females. Why? They can carry more pups. The larger female hammerheads hang out in the middle of schools. A male will push through the crowd and pick one he likes. Usually, the male bites the female until she agrees to mate.

The reproductive cycle occurs once a year. A litter of hammerheads is usually 12 to 14 pups. However, the great hammerhead can produce up to 40 pups at a time. After birth, the parents pay no attention to the baby sharks. Instead, the pups swim off together to warmer water. They stay in the group until they are ready to survive alone.

AD SHARK

SHARK BITE *Hammerheads' mouths are relatively small. This may be why they do so much of their feeding on the sea floor.*

It is possible to distinguish between some common hammerheads by looking at those strange heads.

SHARK BITE *The great hammerhead—the largest species—has a relatively straight front with a small notch in the center.*

Scalloped hammerhead

The bonnethead is the easiest to identify: its head looks more like a shovel than a hammer!

The smooth hammerhead is curved in the front without a center indentation.

NOW THAT'S USING YOUR HEAD

A hammerhead uses its flat, wide head to pin a delicious stingray to the sea floor. It then eats the shocked creature.

The fins of certain hammerheads are a key ingredient in the delicacy known as shark fin soup. As a result, in the past quarter century, the population of these hammerheads has dropped more than 90 percent in the northwest Atlantic Ocean and up to 70 percent in the eastern Pacific and southwest Indian Oceans. (Many other shark species are also at risk for the same reason.) The sharks may have the last laugh, however: recently, it was discovered that a toxin quite harmful to humans is present in shark fin soup and other shark-based items ingested by people. It turns out that the bioaccumulation of mercury in their bodies is toxic to people eating their fins.

In 2007, it was proven that a female bonnethead, in the aquarium at the Henry Doorly Zoo in Nebraska, gave birth with no male partner. The birth had taken place in 2001, but it took some years for DNA technology to explain what had happened. This style of reproduction is known as *parthenogenesis*, in which an egg cell automatically becomes an embryo. The phenomenon had been witnessed previously in bony fish, but this was the first occurrence in cartilaginous fish (having a skeleton composed of cartilage).

SAND TIGER

SHARK BITE *A sand tiger shark can have more than 3,000 of those terrifying teeth over the course of its lifetime.*

SHARK

The sand tiger's 85 to 94 ragged, triangular teeth, visible even when its mouth is closed, give the shark a very menacing look. And it is not totally undeserved. Those jagged, spike-like teeth and the shark's large, bulky body make the sand tiger potentially dangerous to humans. Spearfishers and anyone else who might provoke a sand tiger are particularly at risk.

Adding to the shark's unique appearance are small eyes—yellow with a black pupil—that lack the nictitating eyelid (which sharks pull over their eyes for protection).

This shark can be found in warmer coastal seas worldwide, except for the eastern Pacific Ocean. It is especially common on the U.S. eastern seaboard, Argentina, South Africa, Japan, and Australia. The sand tiger is often located in the surf area near the beach, which is how this shark got its name.

The sand tiger is the only shark species known to come to the surface and gulp air. It then holds the air in its stomach, allowing the shark to float motionless and surprise prey. (This shark is more dense than water, so without this trick, it would sink to the bottom.) Its prey, which is often swallowed whole, can include bony fish, squid, rays, crabs, lobsters, and smaller sharks.

Sand tigers hunt at night, and have been known to travel in small or large groups, especially when feeding on schools of fish.

Female sand tigers give birth to only one or two pups at a time. Why such a small litter? Read more about sand tigers in Shark Attacks on page 64.

SHARK STATS

LENGTH 4–10.5 feet

WEIGHT 200–350 lbs

RANGE Temperate and tropical oceans, except for the eastern Pacific

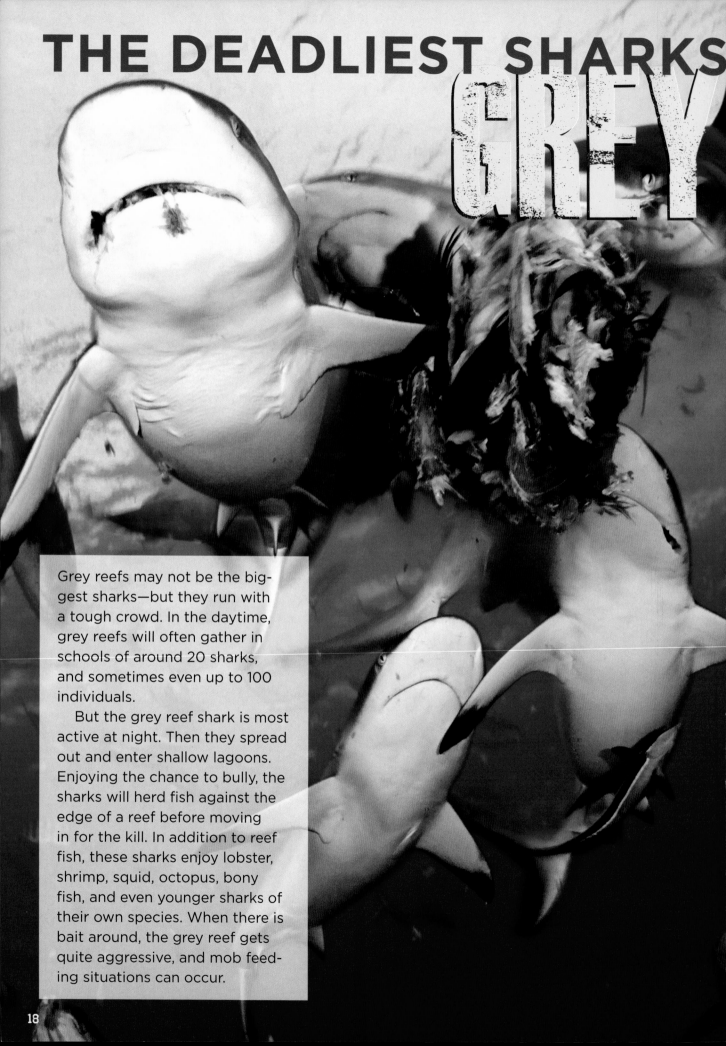

THE DEADLIEST SHARKS
GREY

Grey reefs may not be the biggest sharks—but they run with a tough crowd. In the daytime, grey reefs will often gather in schools of around 20 sharks, and sometimes even up to 100 individuals.

But the grey reef shark is most active at night. Then they spread out and enter shallow lagoons. Enjoying the chance to bully, the sharks will herd fish against the edge of a reef before moving in for the kill. In addition to reef fish, these sharks enjoy lobster, shrimp, squid, octopus, bony fish, and even younger sharks of their own species. When there is bait around, the grey reef gets quite aggressive, and mob feeding situations can occur.

REEF SHARK

SHARK BITE *Grey reef sharks who live near ocean reefs like to travel around, often quite long distances. But the sharks who settle near lagoons tend to stay put, returning to the same area each day.*

Most common in the Indo-Pacific, the grey reef shark is often found around coral reefs.

Humans should keep their distance from grey reef sharks. However, they'll generally attack only if threatened or cornered. And they'll even give fair warning. The threatened grey reef raises its snout, lowers its side fins, arches its back, and sways back and forth while swimming. It may then deliver a fast bite and quickly retreat.

After a 12-month pregnancy, female grey reef sharks will give birth to a small litter—only one to six pups.

SHARK STATS

LENGTH Up to 7 feet

WEIGHT 75 lbs

RANGE Indian and Pacific Oceans, coral reefs

SHORTFIN MA

SHARK BITE *Authors have often been inspired by the fearsome mako. The shark has been featured as a "villain" in the works of adventure novelist Zane Grey, in the classic fishing tale* The Old Man and the Sea *by Ernest Hemingway, and even in* Finding Nemo.

KO SHARK

SHARK STATS

LENGTH 6–12 feet

WEIGHT Up to 1,000 lbs

RANGE Every ocean

With its pointed snout, streamlined body, and shiny bright-blue coloration, the mako shark is truly a thing of beauty. But it is also a thing of death.

The mako is big, aggressive, and powerful. But being big doesn't slow down this shark. The shortfin mako is one of the world's fastest sharks, reaching speeds up to 40 miles per hour. And they can jump, too—leaping up to 20 feet in the air.

The mako needs to eat the equivalent of 3 percent of its body weight every day. This is bad news for the bony fish, porpoises, turtles, and birds it encounters. The mako swims below its prey and then lunges upward. With its narrow, hooked, razor-sharp teeth, the mako makes quick work of its victims.

These sharks are found in all the world's oceans. And they don't stay in one place. It is not uncommon for a mako to swim more than 1,000 miles in search of food. Like its relative the great white, the mako can raise its body temperature above the water temperature, so it can remain active in different settings.

Swimming in a figure-8 pattern with its mouth open, the mako is an intimidating creature. And it doesn't give up without a fight. Boats have been damaged and fishermen injured by mako sharks even after the sharks were caught and reeled in.

Want a tip for spotting the whitetip? Simple: look for the white tips on its fins. Even without this distinctive coloration, the oceanic whitetip's fins give the shark a unique look. The dorsal (top) fin is large and rounded. The pectoral (side) fins are strangely long and wing-like.

It's mainly a quiet life for the oceanic whitetip, swimming slowly and alone in deep, open waters. But things change in a hurry when disaster strikes—and this is what makes the oceanic whitetip so deadly. When a plane crashes or ship starts to sink way out in the ocean, whitetips move in for the kill—lots of whitetips. They are usually the first to arrive on the scene. And a feeding frenzy commences.

Divers must also beware. Due to the wide-open waters of its habitat, the whitetip is curious about any potential food source it happens upon. This is often tuna, marlin, birds, turtles, and snails.

Two odd feeding techniques have been observed in oceanic whitetips. In one instance, the shark approached a school of fish and slowly took bites out of it. In another situation, the whitetip lazily swam through a school of tuna with its mouth open, catching the fish. Whitetips have pointier teeth on their lower jaws and broad, triangular, serrated upper teeth.

Oceanic whitetips have been known to swim along with groups of pilot whales. The reason for this isn't clear. It may be related to the whales' ability to find squid, which whitetips also like to eat.

The young sharks often have dark markings on their white tips.

SHARK STATS

LENGTH 10 feet

WEIGHT 350 lbs

RANGE Tropical and sub-tropical waters throughout the world

THE DEADLIEST SHARKS
OCEANIC WHI

SHARK BITE *Hunting whitetips for their fins, for sharkfin soup, has led to a dramatic decline in their population. Whitetips are now classifed as vulnerable across the world, and critically endangered in some places.*

TETIP SHARK

TIGER SHARK

SHARK BITE *Tiger sharks have quite the reputation as garbage eaters: tires, nails, bottles, and much more have been found in their stomachs.*

Young tiger sharks are fairly easy to identify, thanks to the dark spots and vertical stripes that have given the species its name. But don't get over-confident, as these markings fade over time. Be very cautious of the tiger shark. It is second only to the great white in verified attacks on humans. No wonder, like the great white, it also has the nickname "maneater shark."

You can find the tiger shark in the open ocean, but it seems to prefer murkier coastal waters around the world. It hunts at night, all alone, moving stealthily inshore. Because of their imposing size, adult tiger sharks have almost no natural predators.

The tiger shark's large, very sharp teeth come in handy when attacking larger prey. And it has a unique mouth. In most sharks with similar feeding patterns, the lower jaw holds the prey in place and the upper jaw does the cutting. Not so with the tiger shark. Both jaws have rows of 24 identical teeth, top and bottom. Different sections of the tooth cut and saw into the prey.

The tiger shark's diet is the most diverse of all sharks. Common prey includes turtles, rays, birds, squid, dolphins, and sharks. But the tiger shark will eat just about anything.

SHARK STATS

LENGTH 16–18 feet

WEIGHT 850–1,400 lbs

RANGE Every ocean

Tiger sharks have an interesting relationship with the dugong, a large, lumbering marine mammal related to the manatee. Dugongs love seagrass, and tiger sharks love dugongs—love eating them. (One study showed that a tiger shark will gladly pick a dugong over a dolphin.) Shark Bay in Australia got its name because of all the tiger sharks, who showed up because of all the dugongs. So these dugongs have slowly adjusted their behavior: they seem to forage for seagrass in deeper waters, where tiger sharks are less likely to go. Also, dugongs come to the surface more often when they know sharks are around, likely to scan the area for safety.

The tiger shark's massive appetite increases the risk to humans. They are less likely to bite and release, as other shark species do.

The tiger's mating ritual is not too much fun for the female. The male will bite her on her fins or back, holding her in place. Serious scars are often found on female tiger sharks. They become pregnant only about once every three years; the pain of the process may be a contributing factor.

The average litter size is around 40 pups. They start out with long tails that slow down their swimming. The distinctive markings on the young may serve as camouflage. Tiger shark pups stay close to shore, near the surface. The lines may help them blend in with the waves.

THE MYTH OF THE TIGER SHARK

Tiger sharks have been mythologized. Early Hawaiians referred to both tiger sharks and great whites as *niuhi*. Women were forbidden to consume *niuhi* meat. Meanwhile, eating the eyes of *niuhi* was believed to give chiefs the power to see the future. Legend has it that the mother of Hawaii's greatest king, Kamehameha I, requested *niuhi* eyes during her pregnancy in 1753, believing that would make her offspring a powerful and brave leader.

GREAT

WHITE SHARK

The name comes from their white bellies and tremendous size. But the first thing that comes to mind when the words "great white" are uttered? Fear. The great white is responsible for more fatal attacks on humans than any other type of shark.

SHARK STATS
LENGTH **13–16 feet**
WEIGHT **1,500–2,500 lbs**
RANGE **Every ocean**

The great white shark is the world's largest predatory animal. The average length of a great white is 15 feet. However, the largest ones can reach lengths of more than 20 feet, and weigh more than 4,000 pounds.

Even though they've been around for 50 million years, great whites remain a mystery, and we still have much to learn about them. They live in oceans around the world, and regularly travel great distances, at average speeds of 10 miles an hour. So these sharks are difficult to track over long periods.

They are also difficult to escape. Great whites are found on coastlines, tropical waters inshore, and far offshore. They're near the surface, or 800 feet below. These sharks are comfortable in warmer waters and cold water (thanks to a circulatory system that keeps body temperature 10 to 20 degrees Fahrenheit above water temperature). From Africa to Australia, East Coast and West Coast of the United States, to the Mediterranean and South America, the great white is at home nearly everywhere.

The great white shark is aided in its endless pursuit of prey by a powerful sense of smell. (They reportedly can detect a tiny amount of blood in water from more than a mile away.) Like all sharks, the great white also has organs known as electroreceptors. These can sense the electrical field given off by living creatures. If you're alive, the great white can find you.

After detection comes the approach, and there is usually no getting away. The great white will vary its attack depending on the situation. It will swim slightly below the surface until it's three feet away and then suddenly leap out of the water at its prey. Or it will begin partially out of the water and rapidly charge at its target. (In a burst of speed, great whites can reach 25 miles per hour.) And then there's always a chance the great white will attack from below. These sharks can swim vertically, getting an excellent view of their prey.

SHARK BITE *Many great whites have scratches and scars on their snouts from their victims. Great whites have the unique ability to roll their eyes back into their heads to protect them from being damaged.*

SHARK CHICKEN

Don't violate a great white's personal space. Two sharks swimming in the same direction will maintain the same distance from each other. And if they are approaching the same prey, it is believed that one great white will give a "heads up" to the other by splashing, rolling, or slapping at the water. The other shark sees or hears the message: Stay away, this meal is mine.

A recent study has proven that great whites are very calculating predators who will intentionally target specific prey. But they do occasionally make mistakes. Typically, when they bite into something that turns out to be unappealing—such as a human being or a boat—they will realize it very quickly and move on.

As a result, most great white bites are not fatal. But they're not pretty. It's a smooth, regulated process: the shark first angles up its snout and drops its lower jaw, literally sizing up the prey. The upper jaw thrusts forward, revealing three-inch-long triangular teeth. The powerful lower jaw snaps up, trapping the prey, narrower bottom teeth holding it in place. The snout drops as the upper teeth slice into the flesh. The great white shakes its head from side to side. If its victim is a seal, sea turtle, whale, or sea bird, it will be eaten. A human might get tossed back.

Great whites are apex predators, at the top of the food chain. No one messes with them, except the occasional killer whale or an even larger shark. The biggest threat comes from humans. Some want the jaws and teeth (for profit), the flesh (for meat), skin (for leather), liver (for oils), and fins (for soup and supplements). Museums want to display full carcasses.

The International Union for Conservation of Nature lists great whites as a vulnerable species. Though great whites are harmful to humans, the threat has been greatly exaggerated since the 1975 release of Steven Spielberg's blockbuster film *Jaws*. The "Jaws effect" has greatly increased reported sightings, sport fishing, and general terror attributed to great whites.

Great whites give birth to live young. Moms will give birth to up to 14 pups at a time, which can each be 5 feet long. And as soon as they're born, great white pups are on their own.

SHARK BITE *Bull sharks have been caught in the Mississippi River as far upstream as Illinois!*

BULL SHARK

Don't try to be a matador when this bull is around. It gets the name from a stocky appearance (with a blunt, rounded snout) and a combative nature. And like its namesake, the bull shark will head-butt its prey before an attack.

Many consider the bull shark to be the world's most dangerous shark. One reason is pretty straightforward: it is the only shark species known to spend a lot of time in fresh water. The bull shark likes warm, shallow water near coastlines, which is coincidentally where people like to swim. In addition, bull sharks are aggressive and big.

Bull sharks hang out in cloudy water, so they're not always identifiable during an attack. So these sharks may be responsible for even more harm than we know.

Their diet usually consists of bony fish, young sharks, and stingrays. The bull shark's eyes are rather small, so sight may not be very important in its hunting. This makes sense, as it often hunts in murky settings.

Bull sharks are generally slow swimmers, but have bursts of speed up to 11 miles an hour.

They live worldwide in warmer coastal waters, coming as far north as Massachusetts in the summer. But bull sharks are also found inland, traveling long distances up rivers and even into lakes.

Pregnant bull sharks migrate to estuaries—partially closed bodies of water—to give birth. The litter is usually six to eight pups. The young stay in the estuary till the water cools; then they move farther offshore.

SHARK STATS

LENGTH 9 feet

WEIGHT 500 lbs

RANGE Shallow coastal waters of the Atlantic and Pacific

WEIRD SHA

S harks can be deadly, and fascinating, and many other things—including... weird. Goofy. Bizarre. And sure, some of them—like our friend the hammerhead—are both terrifying and strange.

Let's take a look at some of the quirkier sharks around. From surprising forms (like a pancake or a snake) to offbeat colors (watch where you step, there's a shark hiding below!) to unique sleeping and eating habits, these are the freakiest finned fellows.

Goblin shark

RKS

SLEEPER SHA

The Pacific sleeper shark can't help the fact that it's so sluggish— it's built that way. With a heavy, cylindrical body, short snout, and very small fins, the sleeper is one of the slowest sharks around. Often found in the very deep sea—sometimes 6,500 feet down—the shark leads a mysterious life. It may sit on the sea floor for long stretches of time, not doing much of anything.

Because prey is not plentiful at such depths, this massive shark (the biggest can grow to lengths of 24 feet) is able to store food in its stomach. When it does eat, the Pacific sleeper, literally, has a big appetite. Its jaws—with spike-like upper teeth and broad lower teeth—are well built for taking large bites out of large, tough prey—even swallowing some fish whole. This may help explain the surprising fact that sleeper sharks are one of the only predators of giant squid. These squid can be twice the size of the sleeper shark! For a mellower meal, Pacific sleeper sharks are known to feed on dead grey whales that sink to the ocean floor. Their finely developed sense of smell helps them locate these rotting carcasses.

RK

SHARK BITE   *The meat of Pacific sleeper sharks is toxic to humans.*

FRILLED SHA

SHARK BITE *Expectant frilled sharks are believed to be pregnant for 42 months! That would be the longest gestation of any known vertebrate species.*

RK

Have you just spotted a small Loch Ness monster? It might actually be the frilled shark (also known as frill shark). This strange, eel-like creature shows up here and there in the Atlantic and Pacific Oceans. It is generally under seven feet long and almost never comes to the surface, so this shark is probably not a mythical sea serpent. Still, it does have an almost primitive appearance: lizard-like head, frilled gills (which give the shark its common name), slender body, and very long caudal (tail) fin. It is likely the descendant of a much larger prehistoric shark.

The frilled shark's relatively large mouth is filled with 300 three-pronged teeth split into 25 rows. (Scientists have accidentally discovered how sharp the teeth are.) This makes it unlikely that prey—often squid—have any chance to escape. It is believed that the frilled shark hovers in the water and then suddenly lunges at its target, attacking much like a snake would.

ANGEL SHA

The angel shark's scientific name, *Squatina*, sounds about right for these sharks that look like they've been flattened. (In Latin, *squatina* just means "a kind of shark.") They actually look more like a stingray than a shark, with wide, flat heads and the "angel wing" pectoral (side) fins. (They are separated from the head, unlike on a ray.) The tail section is at least a bit more shark-like.

Different varieties of angel sharks live in different parts of the world, but they're all bottom-dwellers. During the day, the angel shark will bury itself in the sand or mud. The Pacific angel shark, with its off-white color and little brown and gray splotches, is a great example of sand camouflage. It waits and waits for prey to swim by—halibut, crabs, squid—and then ambushes its victim. The shark traps its prey with powerful jaws and small but sharp, spread-out teeth. Then it returns to hiding to await another meal. No wonder the angel shark has earned the nickname "sand devil."

SHARK STATS

LENGTH 6–8 feet

WEIGHT 75 lbs

RANGE Mostly in shallow, temperate waters

RK

SHARK BITE *Angel sharks migrate to colder northern waters during the warm summer months.*

If the cookiecutter didn't already exist, it would probably be dreamed up as a perfectly named comic book villain. It's not a big shark—20 inches long at most—but the cookiecutter is one of the sneakiest killers. They live in deep water during the day. At night, they move toward the surface in search of unsuspecting prey. The shark actually glows brightly, except for a dark collar around its throat. From underneath, it's believed that this dark patch looks like the shadow of a small fish. So a larger fish such as a marlin or tuna—or even a dolphin, shark, seal, or whale—comes by thinking it has happened upon an easy meal.

That's when the cookie-cutter attacks. With large, suction-like lips and pointy upper teeth, it suddenly attaches itself to the prey. The cookiecutter spins, cutting out a hole of flesh with its very large, triangular bottom teeth. The resulting wound is a gaping circular hole—shaped just like a cookie.

SHARK STATS

LENGTH Up to 20 inches

WEIGHT 7-10 lbs

RANGE Tropical and warm-temperate oceans around the world; found near large islands

WEIRD SHARKS
COOKIECUTT

SHARK BITE A 2011 study revealed the first cookiecutter attack on a living human— and the shark made repeated attacks. So night swimmers should definitely beware.

ER SHARK

WEIRD SHARKS
NURSE SHARK

SHARK BITE *Nurse sharks will often return to the same resting spot after a night of hunting, typically in the crevices in rocks or reefs.*

In the unlikely event that you get bitten by a nurse shark, your actual nurse better have surgical instruments on hand to release the vice-like jaws of this shark.

It is unlikely, though: this funny-looking shark—with two barbel "whiskers" hanging down and a very long tail fin—is considered pretty lazy. During the day, they just loaf around on the sandy sea floor. Often a group of nurse sharks will pile on top of one another.

At night, they're more active, swimming slowly around or just crawling along the sea floor using their pectoral (side) fins. With such small mouths, biting isn't really their style. Instead, with a muscular pharynx, they suck in their food. This might be fish, octopus, squid, lobster, or shrimp. Nurse sharks have been known to flip over a shell and suck out the snail within.

Several males will try to mate with the same female nurse shark, biting her pectoral fins to hold her in place. The females must get fed up with this, as they will often retreat to shallow water and hide their fins in the sand.

SHARK STATS

LENGTH 8–14 feet

WEIGHT 200–330 lbs

RANGE Waters around Central America and Carribean islands

45

Maybe it's good that it is so dark in the deep sea, because this is an ugly-looking shark. You can partially blame an incredibly long, flat, trowel-shaped snout. Also, its body is mostly pink. This is caused by blood vessels under its nearly see-through skin.

With its dark, undersea habitat, the goblin relies on sensors throughout its tremendous snout to locate prey—shrimp, octopus, fish, and squid. When it does, the shark's jaws shoot forward quickly like a catapult, not improving its overall appearance. The teeth are narrow: 26 on the top and 24 below. And the goblin's gobbling commences.

Though known to live all over the world, the goblin shark is rarely seen, so it remains a true mystery of the deep.

SHARK STATS

LENGTH Up to 11 feet

WEIGHT Up to 350 lbs

RANGE Coast of Japan, Gulf of Mexico, and elsewhere in the Pacific and Atlantic Oceans

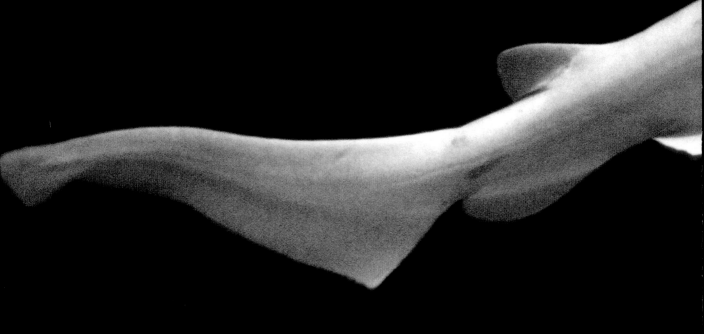

WEIRD SHARKS
GOBLIN SH

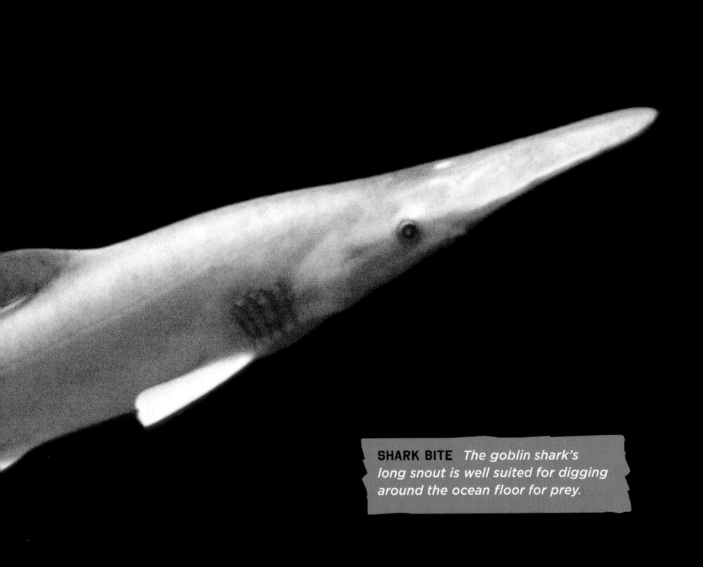

SHARK BITE *The goblin shark's long snout is well suited for digging around the ocean floor for prey.*

ARK

SPOTTED WO

Looking like a bloated snake, the spotted wobbegong is another shark content to chill out on the ocean floor. With its yellow, green, and brown coloring and white O-shaped markings on its back, the shark is reminiscent of army camouflage. The wide, flat body and hanging tassels add to the creature's unique look.

Female wobbegongs release pheromones into the water to attract the males.

These sharks are not much risk to humans, but they are sometimes stepped on due to their excellent camouflage. And if you do happen to not notice it, blended into the sandy bottom, and step on a wobbegong, it will very likely bite your foot in return.

The wobbegong hunts by night, if it can be called hunting. The shark will often wait for prey to come close to its mouth. A meal might be bony fish, crab, lobster, or octopus. Prey has even been observed to chew on the wobbegong's tassels before being consumed. When feeling more energetic, the wobbegong will sneak up on prey from a long way away.

SHARK STATS

LENGTH 5–6 feet

WEIGHT 45–50 lbs

RANGE Shallow waters in East Indian Ocean, southern Australia, western Queensland

BBEGONG

SHARK BITE *The word "wobbegong" comes from the aboriginal Australian for "shaggy beard."*

ZEBRA SHARK

SHARK BITE *In India, these sharks are known as "monkey mouth sharks."*

The name zebra shark makes much more sense when they're young. These sharks start out darkly colored with prominent white stripes. As they age, the coloring changes to yellowish with brown spots. So they do have the logical nickname of "leopard shark."

The adults, who usually grow to less than eight feet long, also develop deep ridges along their bodies.

The caudal (tail) fin is almost as long as the rest of the body.

A bottom dweller, at night, it navigates through crevices looking for snails, shrimp, crabs, and fish.

It spends the days casually resting on the sandy floor. The zebra shark is known to prop itself up on its side fins while facing the current with its mouth open. They do this to help force oxygen-rich water through their mouth and spiracles (breathing holes) and over their gills. The zebra shark's spiracles, which are directly behind the eyes, are as big as or bigger than the eyes.

SHARK STATS

LENGTH 5–8 feet
WEIGHT 150 lbs
RANGE Tropical coastal waters

The horn shark may seem like a sleepy, mellow, West Coast dude, but watch out for its spines. With sharp, white spines (which give the shark its name) on its top fins, the horn shark makes it clear it does not want you to bother it. You can end up with a nasty puncture wound. Still not getting the message? Okay, it will bite your finger, too.

It hangs out in underwater caves, crevices, and kelp forests during the day. (It is comfortable down there, because the horn shark's eyes are sensitive to the light.) The muddy brown body color is good camouflage for this small shark. A horn shark is content to live in the same general area its entire life.

Not much of a swimmer, the horn shark will sometimes push itself along the sea floor with its strong fins. It seeks out crabs, shrimp, and mollusks. When the horn shark catches something, sharp front teeth hold the prey in place, and flat back teeth grind it up. (Its scientific name, *Heterodontus,* is Greek for "different teeth.")

The horn shark has a specific mating ritual. In December or January, the male will chase the female. When she's ready, they both fall to the sea floor. The male bites the female's pectoral (side) fin and inserts a clasper into her cloaca opening. This process takes about half an hour.

Over the next three to four months, the female will lay eggs, two at a time, every 12 days or so.

HORN SHARK

GOOD EGGS

Horn sharks take care of their young. The 5-inch egg case is spiral-shaped, and is easily wedged into a crevice for protection. Meanwhile, the kelp-like coloring of the egg case provides camouflage. It hatches after about six to nine months.

SHARK BITE *If a horn shark's diet consists of purple sea urchins, its spines will turn purple.*

PREHISTO

There are some sharks we don't need to worry about at all. But that's only because they are long extinct. However, many of their traits are carried on in the sharks of today. Fossil records indicate that sharks have been around for at least 420 million years. That's more than 200 million years before the first dinosaurs roamed the Earth. Let's take a look at just a few of these ancient creatures of the deep.

MEGALODON

Though it's been gone for more than a million years, megalodons can still strike fear in our hearts. The name comes from the Greek for "big tooth." With a diagonal length of more than seven inches, these razor-sharp triangular teeth are the biggest of any recorded shark. Which is fitting for the largest shark in history. Using fossilized teeth and vertebra, scientists have estimated a total length between 50 and 70 feet, with a weight somewhere between 50 and 100 tons. Megalodons, which date back at least 25 million years, would eat anything and everything, from fish and squid to dolphins and whales.

CLADOSELACHE

Though dating back 370 million years, paleontologists have a surprisingly solid understanding of cladoselache. That's because excellent fossilized specimens were found outside of Cleveland, Ohio. This was a fast, streamlined, three- to six-foot shark that likely swallowed prey whole. Interestingly, the cladoselache lacked scales on most of its body. But even more interesting, the male cladoselache also lacked claspers, the organ used in reproduction. Scientists are still puzzling over that one.

STETHACANTHUS

Stethacanthus, which lived approximately 360 million years ago, was in many ways your average shark: scales, sharp teeth, sleek body. Except it also had an ironing board sticking out of its back. This bizarre protrusion in this not-quite-three-foot shark, which has also been compared to an anvil, may have been a "docking port" with the female during mating.

SHARK ATTA

We know that sharks don't hunt for people. We don't taste particularly good to them. And if they happen to mistake us for a sea turtle or something less bony and more interesting, they typically spit us out after the first bite. So most shark attacks are not fatal. But they do happen—and when they do, they're a grisly affair.

World War II, July 26, 1945: The Navy ship *Indianapolis* made a crucial delivery to the U.S. base on the island of Tinian in the Pacific Ocean. Parts were received to complete the first atomic bomb to be used in combat history.

July 30, shortly after midnight: Sailing toward the island of Leyte, where the crew would receive new training, the *Indianapolis* was struck by two torpedoes from a Japanese submarine. The hits caused major damage, and the mighty warship began to sink. Of 1,196 people aboard, about 900 initially survived and ended up in the water. There were very few lifeboats, so most used life jackets to stay afloat. With almost no food or drinkable water, they prayed for rescue.

July 30, sunrise: Shark attacks began. It was likely oceanic whitetips; perhaps some tiger sharks. Late afternoons and nights were the worst for the next several days. Screams would punctuate the quiet and all knew that another crewman had lost the battle with the sharks.

August 2–3: A plane and then a ship arrived to pull out survivors. The shark attacks had continued right up until that point—the most shark attacks on humans in history. "There'd be 15 or 20 [sharks] and they'd swim around your group, just keep swimming around," said survivor Giles McCoy. "If anybody went out of the group, [the sharks would] grab their feet and just take them. You'd never see them again." Most deaths were likely not caused directly by sharks, but rather by exposure to the elements and lack of food and water. But then sharks dragged off the bodies.

Of the original 900 survivors, only 321 were alive to be pulled from the water, and of those, 317 survived. It remains the worst maritime disaster in U.S. naval history.

ANAPOLIS

SHARK BITE *As a result of this tragedy, the U.S. military began to research shark repellents. They discovered that the smell of dead sharks repelled live ones, as did copper compounds.*

SHARK ATTACKS
JERSEY SHO
1916: INSPIRATION FOR JAWS

SHARK BITE *This story of a quiet town besieged by a killer shark inspired novelist Peter Benchley to write Jaws, which was published in 1974. The rest, as they say, is history....*

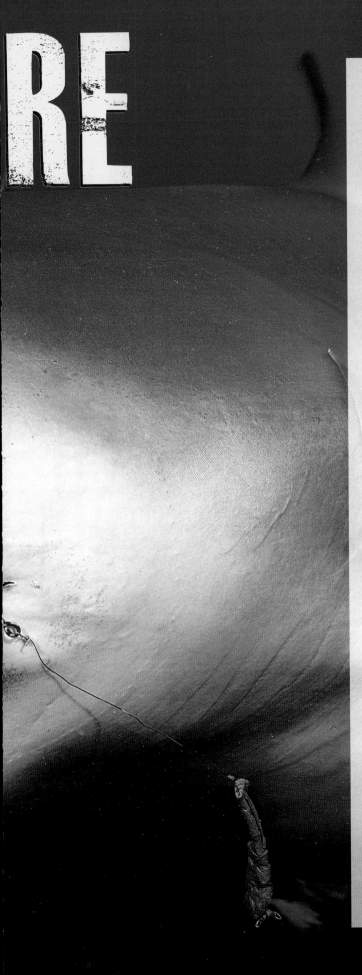

There was an oppressive heat wave during the summer of 1916, and thousands headed to the Jersey Shore seeking relief. On July 1, in Beach Haven, 25-year-old Charles Vasant headed into the Atlantic for a quick swim.

His shouts soon attracted the attention of a lifeguard. A shark was biting at his legs. He was pulled onto shore but the bleeding couldn't be stopped. Vasant died.

It was a tragedy to be sure, but was viewed as a freak occurrence. The season carried on cautiously—for five more days, anyway. Then, at the Spring Lake resort 45 miles to the north, bellboy Charles Bruder went for a dip. Screams again drew rescuers; a shark had bitten off his legs. He bled to death while being brought to shore.

Panic set in throughout the region, but people were relatively calm in Matawan. The sleepy town was 30 miles farther north, not to mention 16 miles inland. So when resident Thomas Cottrell, a sea captain, claimed he'd spotted an eight-foot shark in freshwater Matawan Creek, he was dismissed as a crank. By 2 p.m. on July 12, the town regretted not heeding those warnings. Lester Stillwell, age 11, was horsing around with friends when a shark violently pulled him under the surface. Businessman Stanley Fisher jumped in to save Lester. The shark attacked Stanley as well; he bled to death hours later. Lester's corpse was not found for another two days.

Just a half-hour and half-mile away, Joseph Dunn, 14, was bitten on the leg. He was pulled out and was the only survivor of these attacks.

On July 14, a great white was killed nearby. In its stomach were 15 pounds of human remains. Was this the culprit, or a bull shark, as others have suggested? It remains unclear to this day.

AIR JAWS

Great whites are terrifying enough when they're in the water. The fact that they can propel themselves into the air as well makes them doubly terrifying.

It's called *breaching*—a purposeful jump out of the water. The phenomenon has been more regularly observed in whales. With great white sharks, breaching is generally considered to be a hunting technique. This has been repeatedly observed at Seal Island in False Bay off the coast of South Africa. Cape fur seals swim happily at the surface. From deep below, a great white plots its attack. It swims rapidly upward toward its prey, reaching speeds up to 40 miles an hour. The momentum carries the shark up and out of the water, sometimes 10 feet into the air. Almost half the time, the attack is successful. If not, the chase is on!

Successful or not, breaching is an awesome thing to witness. It is majestic when such an enormous creature—possibly 4,000 pounds—performs these powerful acrobatics. Photographers Chris Fallows and Rob Lawrence were the first to document the behavior in False Bay. They have developed a technique to elicit the behavior. Chris and Rob take a seal decoy and tow it behind their boat, hoping a great white will have some interest and put on a show.

SHARK ON BOARD

In July, 2011, a research boat near Seal Island got an unannounced passenger. The crew had been studying great whites, using sardines as bait. They had attracted four sharks and observed them over the course of an hour. "Next thing I know, I hear a splash and see a white shark breach out of the water, hovering, literally, over the crew member who was chumming [throwing food bait] on the port side," team leader Dorien Schröder told the *Guardian* newspaper. The shark, estimated at more than 1,000 pounds, landed half on and half off the boat. It thrashed its way completely on deck. Water was poured on the shark's gills to keep it alive. Finally, a crane lifted the shark out of the boat and placed it safely back in the water. The boat was significantly damaged, but everyone onboard was okay.

SHARK BITE *Breaching great whites have been known to "cartwheel" back into the water. This is possibly due to body structure. More of a shark's weight is on the front end, making them more likely to land face-first.*

SHARK BITE *Spring and summer seem to be the great whites' breaching season in False Bay. Right around sunrise is the most likely time to witness the behavior.*

SHARK ATTACKS
SAND TIGER

The female sand tiger shark has two uteri and produces many eggs. However, the litters are almost always two shark pups. The reason: a particularly grisly version of survival of the fittest.

It starts out innocently enough, with the shark embryos getting nutrients from their yolk sac, like many creatures do. When the yolk sac is empty, the hungry pup turns to the eggs around itself for nutrition. This alone is not a completely shocking turn of events. Fourteen different shark species are known to practice *intrauterine cannibalism*. In 13 of those cases, the growing embryos eat the unfertilized eggs around them. That's known as *oophagy*—"egg eating."

The sand tiger embryo, with its developing teeth, takes things a drastic step further. It eats both the unfertilized and fertilized eggs. This is referred to as *adelphophagy*, which translates to "eating one's brother." The stronger embryos survive, until there is only one pup left in each uterus.

Gestation lasts (for the two survivors, anyway) for eight to nine months. By the time they are about seven inches long, they have developed teeth and have begun feeding. By 10 inches, they are moving around inside the uterus.

Not very surprisingly, sand tiger shark pups come into the world larger than other baby sharks. Their average length is about three feet. And they often arrive with swollen stomachs!

SHARK
CANNIBALS

SHARK ATTACKS BETHA

Halloween 2003 turned out to be a scary one for teen surfer Bethany Hamilton. With her best friend, Alana, and Alana's brother and dad, she'd gone for an early-morning surf in Kauai, Hawaii. It was business as usual for Bethany. Then 13, she'd been surfing as long as she could remember. Her family members were surfers. Bethany had even been entering competitions since age eight. On this day, she was just relaxing on her surfboard, her left arm dangling in the calm water....

The tiger shark, maybe a 15-footer, came out of nowhere. It latched onto Bethany's left arm—she felt pressure and quick tugs—and it vanished just as quickly. Bright-red blood filled the water. Her arm was gone, just below the shoulder. It is possible the shark mistook Bethany's board for a sea turtle, which are common in those waters off Kauai.

Alana's family helped Bethany paddle back to shore. Alana's dad, thinking fast, made a tourniquet for her out of a surfboard leash. Even so, by the time Bethany was taken to the hospital, she'd lost 60% of her blood. But Bethany was determined, and just three weeks after being attacked, she was surfing again.

NY HAMILTON

SURVIVOR

In 2005, Bethany won the National Scholastic Surfing Association championships,
    For her courage, Bethany won an ESPY and a Teen Choice award. She wrote the book *Soul Surfer* about her experiences. It has been turned into a movie.

DR. ERICH RITTER

If it can happen to Dr. Erich Ritter, it can happen to anyone. One of the leading shark experts, he was recording a program for the Discovery Channel in the Bahamas in April 2002. He was performing an experiment he'd done many times: proving that sharks ignore humans in clear water. Except the water was rather murky that day and filled with dangerous sharks. The marina manager tossed fish in to lure the sharks away from Erich and a network employee. Luck was not on their side: a remora fish grabbed the bait and brought it right back near Erich. A 350-pound bull shark, also after the bait, took a large bite out of Erich's left calf. Extensive surgery saved his leg.

HEATHER BOSWELL

Nineteen-year-old Heather had a job on a research vessel in the South Pacific in the spring of 1994. She and some friends on the crew were taking a break, going for a swim. The water was warm and it couldn't have been more relaxing—until someone yelled "Shark!" A seaman who'd been swimming nearby was bitten, and the shark—possibly a great white—headed for Heather next. It chewed a bit on her right leg. Next, it grabbed her left leg and pulled her below the surface, thrashing back and forth. They came back up; crew members held onto Heather, trying to pull her into the boat while attempting to knock the shark away. She felt a pop. Heather was safe, but her leg

VAUGHN HILL

There was only one general practitioner on the Chatham Islands in New Zealand in 1996. He'd started the job four months earlier. That day, Dr. Pishief learned that Vaughn Hill, a local resident, had been attacked by a shark off a nearby island. The doctor gathered supplies and, with a pilot, hopped in a small plane. Vaughn and a friend had been diving; on the way back up he found himself in the jaws of a 15-foot "white pointer" shark—a great white. Vaughn's friend got him back to shore, but he'd lost nearly half his blood by the time Dr. Pishief arrived. The doctor administered immediate care and got Vaughn to a hospital. He'd lost an arm and was badly injured...but he survived.

ANDREA RUSH

Before seven-year-old Alysha Webster was killed by a shark off Vanuatu's Malekula Island in 2005, her family was unaware of the region's history. Thirteen years earlier, another visitor from New Zealand had a close encounter—but lived to tell about it. It was the summer of 1992, and 21-year-old Andrea Rush was swimming alone at Port Sandwich, near an anchored yacht. All of a sudden, a shark grabbed her, biting Andrea above and below her right knee. Just as suddenly, the shark spat her out. An artery was punctured, but Andrea survived. Young Alysha was not so lucky in those same waters.

When you encounter a shark, you don't want to lose your head. Eric Nerhus, age 41, was diving for abalone (a valuable type of shellfish) in 25-feet-deep waters off Australia. He was looking down at the sea floor, he so didn't notice the great white shark that appeared seemingly out of nowhere. It swallowed Eric's head, right arm, and both shoulders. Thankfully, his left arm was free. Eric used it to gouge at the 10-foot shark's eye. The shark released a little, but bit down again on Eric's face mask, breaking his nose. Eric kept gouging till the shark released him for good. He credits the lead vest in his wetsuit with preventing further damage from the great white's razor sharp teeth.

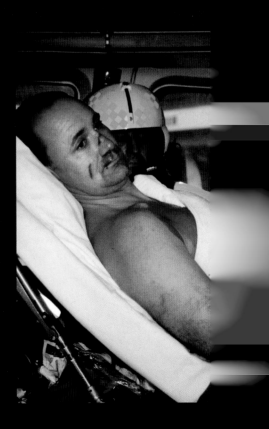

SHARK ATTACKS
DEADLY WAT

There are sharks all over the world, but some areas are clearly "sharkier" than others. Modern technology has given us a much better sense of where sharks are and where they travel. Scientists can now attach a satellite transmitter to a shark's dorsal fin. Information is beamed up to a satellite and back to a computer lab in real time. Of course, to know where sharks are, we can also rely on reports of attacks. Here's a look at the some of the most dangerous shark hot spots on the planet.

ERS

THE RED TRIANGLE

Extending from San Francisco down to Monterey, California, and 30 miles into the Pacific Ocean is the area known as the Red Triangle. It earned its name because there's sometimes blood in the water. This is the likeliest spot on Earth for a human to be attacked by a great white shark. A hundred or more great whites converge here in the late summer every year. They come for their favorite prey, seals, who migrate to the beaches and in the surrounding waters. Needless to say, you do not want to get between a great white and a tasty seal.

FLORIDA COAST

Visit sunny Florida—Disney World! Kennedy Space Center! Volusia County, the Shark Attack Capital of the World! This 47-mile stretch on central Florida's Atlantic coast was the site of 21 percent of the world's shark attacks on humans from 1998 to 2008. And the county has shown no signs of giving up its top spot. The high number of bites is likely due to the great number of swimmers and fisher-men in the water here. The good news is, these are generally minor bites from spinners and blacktips, sharks that are rarely longer than seven feet.

SOUTHERN CALIFORNIA COAST

Laws to protect marine mammals have greatly increased the number of sea lions in southern California. There were about 3,000 in the 1920s but now there's an estimated 250,000. And more sea lions means more hungry great white sharks dining in the area. The stretch between Santa Monica and Malibu is particularly considered a shark hot spot. Marine biologists aren't quite sure why it's is so popular, but it's giving them a greater chance to study the deadly beasts. And swimmers are watching their toes.

great white shark

bull shark

SOUTH AFRICAN COAST

Second Beach at St. John's Port in South Africa has the distinction of being the World's Most Dangerous Beach. In five years, there have been six fatal attacks at the beach, the highest total anywhere in that period of time. These sharks—mostly bull sharks—don't mess around: every shark attack has resulted in a fatality. Locals believe that pollution in the water has riled up these already aggressive sharks. Others feel the sharks are attracted by nearby witch doctors who sacrifice animals and throw their guts into the water.

NEW ZEALAND COAST

New Zealand's sharks are very agreeable—they'll attack you whether you visit the north or the south. Over the years, the Auckland area has had the country's second greatest number of unprovoked attacks. However, this is likely due to the region's sizeable human population, and no attack there thus far has resulted in a death. There have been more attacks—and four fatalities—in the more sparsely populated Otago regions. Blame the ready availability of prey—seals, dolphins, and pilot whales—for attracting the hunters: great whites, makos, and bronze whalers.

shortfin mako

HAWAII

Since 1828, there have been more than 100 unprovoked shark attacks on humans around Hawaii, with eight fatalities. Most of these attacks are split between Maui and Oahu. It doesn't help that there are 40 different species of shark around Hawaii, and much of their preferred prey can be found there: seals, sea turtles, and baby whales. The shark species responsible for most of these attacks is the aggressive tiger shark. Even so, in Hawaiian mythology sharks are often considered to be an *aumakua*, or ancestral spirit.

tiger shark

PAPUA NEW GUINEA

North of Australia sits New Guinea, the world's second largest island. Its eastern half is Papua, New Guinea. Since 1925, there have been around 50 unprovoked shark attacks there, and half of them have been fatal. A wide variety of sharks call Papua, New Guinea home, including hammerheads, silvertips, and tiger sharks. Extensive interaction with divers and fishermen increases the odds of an attack. Then there's the ritual of "shark calling": sharks are lured with a rattle, then lassoed and clubbed to death. But when that goes wrong....

silvertip shark

bull shark

RECIFE, BRAZIL

In the past 80 years in Brazil, 90 people have been attacked by unprovoked sharks, and 21 have died. But why have such a high percentage—more than half the attacks, and two-thirds of the deaths—occurred off the beach town of Recife? And nearly all in the past 20 years? In the 1980s, a port opened south of the city. This blocked an estuary where bull sharks (one of the more aggressive species) would give birth. So the pregnant sharks moved to another estuary. And that one is uncomfortably near Recife's beaches.

SHARK FAC

Sharks are at the top of the food
chain for many reasons. Fascinating
creatures, sharks have had hundreds
of millions of years to evolve into the
super predators that we know today.
What makes a shark a shark? How and why
do they do the things they do? Get ready
to learn it all, from how they travel long
distances to how they use their sixth sense!

TS

sand tiger shark

SHARK BABI

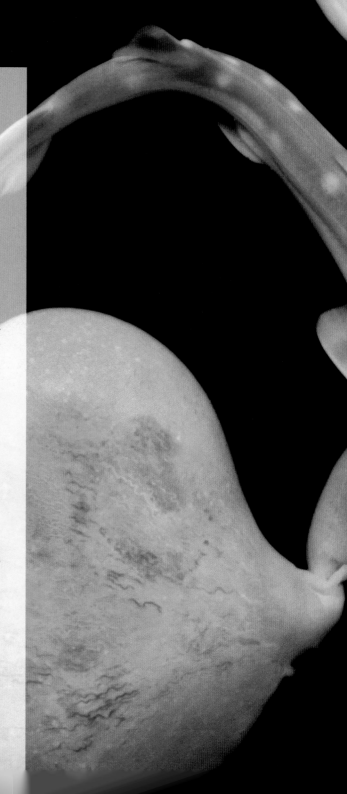

The mating process of sharks isn't completely understood. In different species, interest between males and females—their courtship—seems to be indicated by chasing or a release of pheromones. Biting may also be a sign of interest. However, biting more often seems to be part of the actual mating process: the male will bite the female's fins in order to hold on. Researchers have noticed bite marks on the fins of females in many shark species. It is believed that some species' females have adapted to this behavior by actually growing thicker skin.

Depending on the species, the male and female may curl around each other, or possibly next to each other. The male shark has organs called *claspers*. One of these claspers is inserted into the female's oviduct.

There are three different forms of shark reproduction:

• Most sharks produce eggs that hatch within the mother. The pups are born alive.

• Some sharks lay eggs, which are protected by an egg case. These eggs hatch outside the body.

• Still other sharks produce live young, similar to the way mammals do. The embryo fully develops within the mother.

Litter sizes also vary, from as few as one pup to more than 100.

ES

SHARK BITE The gestation period varies by species, anywhere from five to 24 months.

dogfish shark

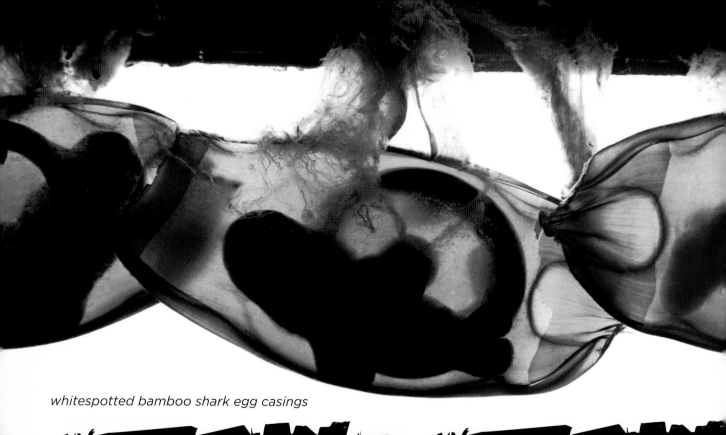

whitespotted bamboo shark egg casings

Though in some species, changes occur as a shark pup grows (coloring, length of tail, etc.), in general shark babies are just smaller versions of the species' adult shark. It's a good thing they're born "fully functional," because once out of the mother, shark pups are almost always on their own. The parents don't raise them in any way.

That being said, some shark mothers do give their kids a fighting chance. They'll give birth in shallow lagoons. Or for those who lay eggs, they sometimes hide the egg cases in camouflaged crevices. The goal is to keep possible predators away from the babies for as

sand tiger shark

lemon shark

long as possible. Those predators are often other sharks, and quite possibly from the same species. Sizes of shark pups vary greatly, and the littlest ones don't stand much of a chance in a hostile environment.

Sometimes a litter of shark pups will stay together in a shallow "nursing area" until they're large enough to strike out on their own. Other times, the shark pup is independent from day one. With luck and instincts, it will survive the slow transition from probable prey—to definite predator.

scalloped hammerhead shark pups

SHARK SEN

Like us, sharks depend on their senses: sight, smell, taste, and hearing. They also have an elaborate sense of touch and a bonus sixth sense. Without the combination of these senses, sharks wouldn't be the highly skilled hunters we know them to be.

TOUCH: Sharks respond to physical contact, but somewhat remarkably, near contact is also noticed. The lateral line is a set of tubes running along a shark's body. There is a main tube on each side of the body from head to tail. If anything comes near the shark, water rushes through pores, into a tube, and over sensory cells. Motion detected!

ELECTRORECEPTION: *The* ampullae of Lorenzini *are a shark's receptor cells, located in the head. They somehow pick up the electrical fields given off by every living organism. It's another handy way for sharks to pinpoint the location of prey.*

SIGHT: *Varies greatly by species. Deeper-dwelling sharks need to see more clearly in the dark. In general, sharks have a wide field of vision (due to having an eye on each side), and can pick up easily on contrasts and slight changes in light levels.*

SMELL: *Highly attuned. Water passes through small nostrils on either side of the snout and over sensory cells. Sharks can tell which direction a smell is coming from. Famously, they can detect tiny bits of blood or chemicals in the water from great distances.*

HEARING: *Very small ear openings on each side of the head lead to a very sensitive inner ear. Sharks are especially good at hearing low frequencies, such as those emitted by injured fish (which are easy prey).*

TASTE: *Sharks definitely have taste buds. This allows for the very common occurrence of "sample biting"—if the victim doesn't taste like something they normally eat, the shark won't take a second bite.*

Carribean reef shark

Modern satellite tracking technology gives scientists a much better understanding of shark migration. Previously, it was thought that sharks remained in the same general area. However, we now know that many sharks migrate, and some regularly travel 1,000 miles or more on a regular basis.

The reasons are similar to other migrating animals: changes in season, availability of prey, and the all-important reproduction process.

SHARK FACTS
SHARK MIGR

ATION

CHANGES IN SEASON

Some sharks, such as the great white and the mako, can raise their body temperature well above the surrounding water's temperature. This ability helps them function in different settings. However, more sharks are cold-blooded: their body temperature is equal to that of the water around them. These sharks need to find waters within their preferred temperature range. Sometimes this might just mean moving deeper or moving closer to the surface. Often it can involve a lengthy journey.

AVAILABILITY OF PREY

Even if seasonal changes don't affect a shark, its prey may react to fluctuations in temperature. Sharks will often follow fish to a new location. An example is in California's infamous Red Triangle: when seals return there in April, you can count on great whites returning there too.

REPRODUCTION PROCESS

Water temperature changes can also be a signal to many sharks that it is time to mate. Sharks will migrate annually to specific mating areas. Then, after gestation, females will migrate to breeding grounds to give birth. These locations are often in shallow-water estuaries to provide shark pups with some safety from predators.

HOW DO THEY GET WHERE THEY'RE GOING?

Sharks don't have GPS, and a lot of the ocean looks pretty much the same. So how do sharks know where they're going, and how do they arrive at the same exact locations year after year? This has puzzled scientists for quite a while. Studies have indicated that sharks' sensors can pick up on the Earth's magnetic fields. The sharks use these fields as a navigation technique.

CAVES OF SLEEPING SHARKS

The often repeated myth is that if a shark stops swimming, it dies. This is based on factual information: for most sharks, motion can genuinely help them breathe. But do they ever get a chance to rest? It's believed that many sharks can "turn off" their brains while still swimming, to reduce overall energy use. Other sharks can remain basically still but face the current (sometimes with open mouths) so oxygen-rich water will run over their gills.

And then there are the Caves of Sleeping Sharks. In 1969, a diver discovered this area in Isla Mujeres, Mexico. There were reef sharks within lying motionless. Researchers soon learned that the water in the caves was high in oxygen and low in salt. The conditions made it very easy for the sharks to breathe without moving. Another benefit of the reduced saltiness: it makes it easier for shark-sucking remora fish to remove parasites from sharks' skin. So the caves provided both relaxation and a good cleaning, like a rest stop with a built-in car wash.

Carribean reef shark

SHARK TAL

Scientists are continually intrigued by sharks, as there is still so much to learn. Technology has sped up the discovery process. Meet the people doing amazing work—which is sometimes quite dangerous—with these ever-mysterious creatures. Say hello to a gigantic shark and a bizarre one. And learn the secrets of shark skin!

JAWS COMES

Dr. Greg Skomal, an accomplished marine biologist, runs the Massachusetts Shark Research Program. He believes that a huge increase in the Cape Cod gray seal population has brought great white sharks back to the region after a long absence.

Greg wanted to study these sharks and their migratory patterns. With the crew of the *Ezyduzit* boat, he located six North Atlantic whites. A professional harpooner helped him safely attach Pop-Up Satellite Archival Transmitting tags to five of the sharks. (The sharks were given nicknames such as Curly, Ruthless, and Storm.) The tags record water temperature, depth, and light. With this information, scientists can estimate a shark's route.

Tagged in early September, the sharks initially remained local, and then began moving south. By mid to late October, they'd reached North Carolina. By early December, they'd made it to northern Florida.

Depths would vary daily, from the surface to below 100 feet. Though generally swimming at depths of 150 feet or less, one shark revealed itself to be quite the diver. For 10 days while off the North Carolina coast, this shark regularly dove to depths as far as 1,500 feet. The range of water temperature during such a dive would be anywhere from 45 degrees Fahrenheit to more than 80 degrees.

"The most surprising thing for me is to find out that these sharks are closely associated with the Continental Shelf, and that association may tell us more about their mating and feeding habits," Greg said. "While this is a small sample of data, the information provides some first insights and glimpses into where these sharks are traveling to and may point to a well-defined migration route."

Curly with his tag

HOME

Curly gets tagged.

SHARK TALES
MEET CURLY

Even for a shark expert like Greg Skomal, it's not every day that you spot an 18-foot great white. Certainly not in the Atlantic Ocean. It was the first great white to be filmed underwater in the Atlantic in 30 years. Tagging and tracking such a shark would be another challenge.

They nicknamed him Curly. At least, they thought Curly was a "him." Upon closer inspection, they changed their minds. "Getting a confirmed female on the research project was really exciting," Greg said. "Up to this point, getting good information on the sexes of our tagged sharks has been a problem." Based on Curly's size, they determined she was mature—probably about 20 years old. Greg had one more theory about Curly. "She was a mystery to me," he said. "Was she pregnant? Where will she give birth? Will she tell me? I wanted answers and hoped the tag would deliver them."

Curly was attracted toward the boat by a floating whale carcass, out of which she quickly took several giant bites. Temporarily losing interest in the whale, Curly began to circle the boat. Greg kept a close eye on her, and when he had the chance, tagged her himself.

Even after being tagged, Curly lingered near the boat. So Greg and cameraman Nick Caloyianis entered a shark cage to photograph and film her up close. Curly went back to the whale for a few more bites, and then turned her attention toward the cage. While attacking the orange buoys connected to the top, Curly somehow became trapped above the cage. She attempted to wildly thrash her way loose, breaking the cage and popping open its door in the process. It was quite the adrenaline rush for Greg and Nick.

Curly finally freed herself. She was already proving to be a worthwhile tagged specimen!

SHARK SKIN

Sharkskin suits aren't actually made from shark skin. However, underwater robots may someday wear suits made out of real shark skin. Real artificial shark skin, that is.

Harvard University professor George Lauder and graduate student Johannes Oeffner wanted to unlock some of the secrets of sharks' speedy swimming ability. So they conducted an experiment. First, they obtained actual skin from large mako sharks. They put the skin on a basic, flexible robot which could mimic a shark's movements. Next they staged "time trials" in a water tank, comparing the shark skin with other materials.

The shark skin won, and George and Johannes think they know why. It's due to the scales, called *denticles*, on a shark's skin. These scales are very sharp and tooth-like. And when moving through the water, they actually create tiny whirlpools. This helps propel the shark along rapidly. Birds and insects use a similar phenomenon when flying.

George believes the development of artificial shark skin could be very beneficial to underwater research. At the very least, it will probably speed up the process!

WHIRLPOOLS

CYCLOPS SHA

an adult dusky shark

It had to be a PhotoShop hoax, right? Pisces Fleet Sportfishing, out of Cabo San Lucas, Mexico, had posted photos on their blog, and they went absolutely viral. So cute! So creepy! But it couldn't be real... could it?

A cyclops shark?

And yet, it was real: a one-eyed shark fetus. Its mother was a dusky shark, caught in the Sea of Cortez. The fetus was found within her.

The cyclops shark was 22 inches long. The eye, in the middle of its head, was determined to be functional. This is a clear indication of cyclopia, a rare birth disorder. It has been observed previously in horses, sheep, pigs, chickens, and even humans.

Researchers believe that had the fetus lived, it would not have survived for long outside of its mother.

"This is extremely rare," shark expert Felipe Galvan Magana told the Pisces Fleet blog. "As far as I know, less than 50 examples of an abnormality like this have been recorded."

ENDANGER

Due to unregulated fishing and the increased demand for shark fins, more than 100 shark species are in trouble. That's about one-fourth of the total number of species. Sharks classified as critically endangered by the International Union for Conservation of Nature (IUCN) have global populations that have decreased, or will decrease, by at least 80 percent in just 10 years or three generations. So some of these species may already be extinct. With the continuing rapid depletion of shark populations, more species may be joining these lists all the time.

ED SHARKS

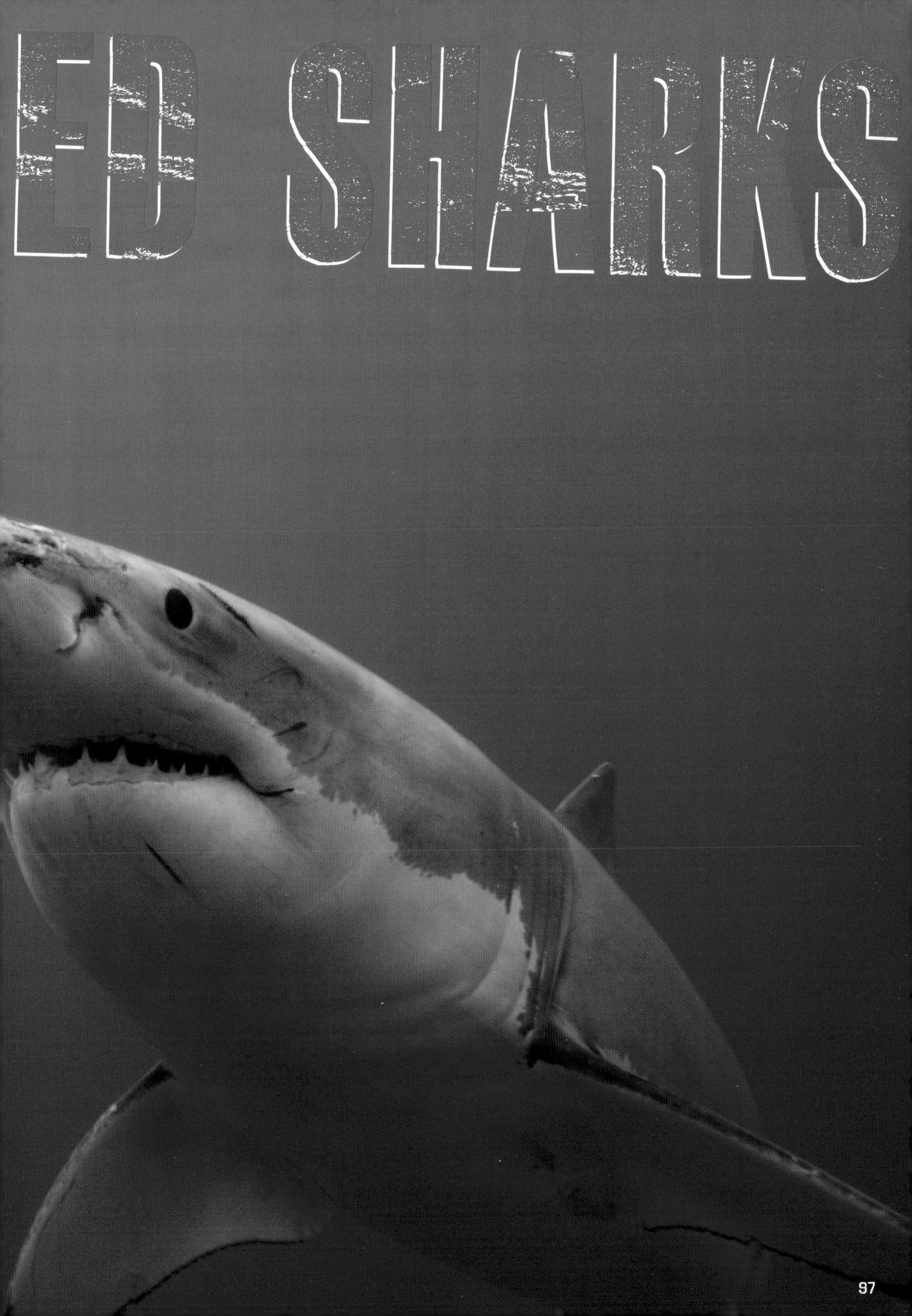

ENDANGERED SHARKS
CRITICALLY

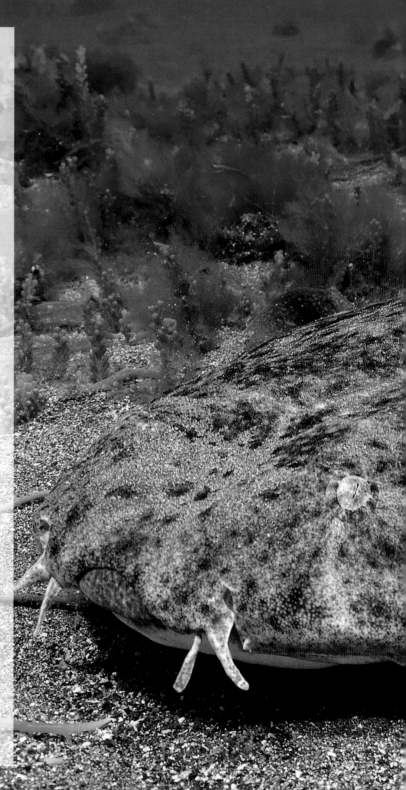

The following sharks are listed as critically endangered:

Pondicherry shark
Small and stocky, this shark was once common inshore in the Indo-West Pacific region. No living specimen has been seen since 1979. Its former habitat has been overrun with unregulated fisheries. This shark likely grew to a length of less than four feet, with a pointed snout, and about 143 rows of teeth on each side of the jaw, upper and lower.

Ganges shark
Though its range might be wider, this shark has only been spotted in India's Ganges-Hooghly River system. Fishing, pollution, and construction of dams have been major threats to this species. With the positioning of its small eyes, it seems this under-seven-foot shark swims along the bottom and looks for prey above that is highlighted by the sun. The Ganges shark has been blamed for attacks on humans, but this has not been verified.

New Guinea river shark
Despite its name, this shark has only been seen off northern Australia. A 2002 survey of its

ENDANGERED

known habitat turned up no specimens of the shark. Adults, which grow to lengths of more than eight feet, seem to prefer murkier inshore waters. It is believed there are fewer than 250 mature living specimens of this shark in the wild.

Irrawaddy River shark
All we know of this shark comes from one specimen found in the late 19th century, in Myanmar's Irrawaddy River. The river is badly polluted, and the mangrove forests where the shark might live have been depleted for fuel and construction materials. It is believed the shark could've grown to lengths of 10 feet. This shark is noted for having very small eyes, a common trait of fish-eaters in murky rivers.

Angel sharks
The species angel shark, sawback angel shark, and smoothback angel shark are all listed as critically endangered. In addition, the Argentine, Taiwan, spiny, and angular varieties are classified as endangered. Angel sharks occur around in the world in temperate and tropical waters, generally in shallow areas. Heavy fishing of these species really began in the late 1970s.

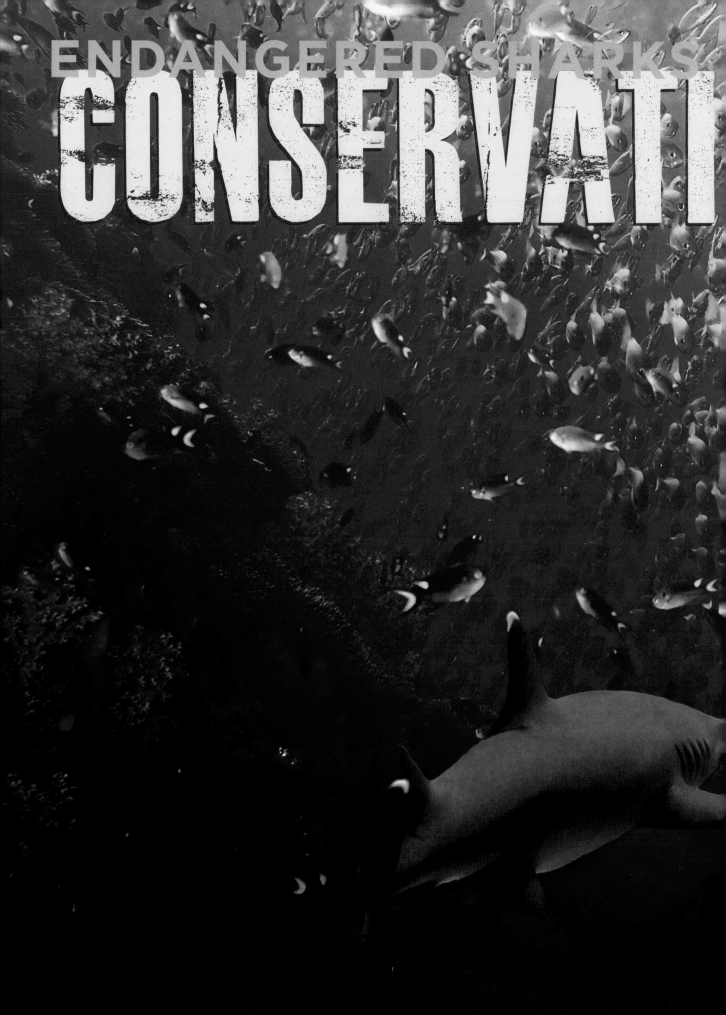

ENDANGERED SHARKS
CONSERVATI

ON EFFORTS

We attack sharks much more than sharks have ever attacked us. Due to vastly increased shark fishing and the mad desire for shark fins—for soup and dietary supplements—shark populations have dropped drastically over the past several decades. Up to 73 million sharks are killed each year as a result of finning, bycatch (when sharks are caught in nets targeting other kinds of fish), and other targeted fishing for sharks. With relatively small litters and slow maturity, the species are simply unable to replenish themselves.

Thankfully, around the globe, passionate individuals and organizations have been attempting to turn the tide. They are pressuring nations and the fishing industry to change their ways, to make sure regulations are followed, and to close loopholes.

In 2010, the U.S. passed the Shark Conservation Act. This act ended shark finning in U.S. waters. It was an enhancement of the Shark Finning Prohibition Act, signed into law in 2000. The U.S. is committed to persuading other nations to enact similar legislation.

Also in 2010, the International Commission for the Conservation of Atlantic Tunas banned the fishing of six hammerhead varieties and the oceanic whitetip shark in the Atlantic. The group also stated that the sharks cannot be kept even if caught accidentally.

In 1991, South Africa became the first nation to label the great white shark as a protected species. The shark is now also protected in New Zealand, Malta, Australia, Namibia, Israel, and in California and Florida in the United States.

Perhaps profit will motivate more shark conservation efforts. A recent study by the R.J. Dunlap Marine Conservation Program determined that a single living reef shark is worth $73 a day in tourist revenue, compared to a one-time price of $50 for the shark's fins.

Are there more sharks in protected waters than in unprotected waters? Researchers from Stony Brook University in New York wanted to answer that question. So they set up 200 "chum cams"—baited underwater video cameras—in the Caribbean. They monitored both marine reserves and unprotected areas. The results were encouraging: sharks were spotted four times as often in the protected zones.

EXTREME

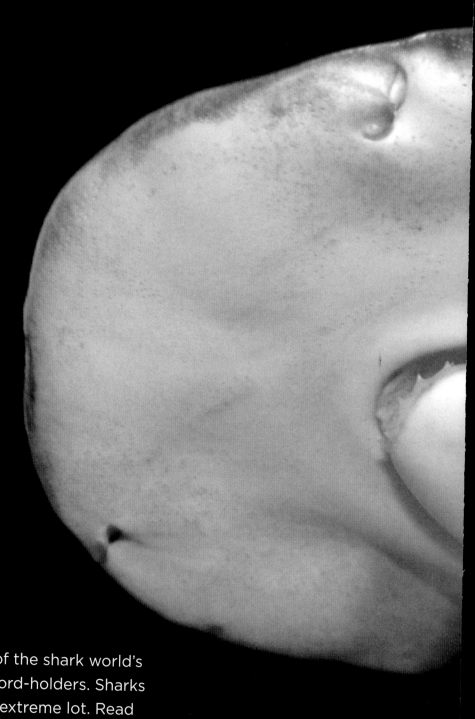

Take a look at some of the shark world's most impressive record-holders. Sharks are already a pretty extreme lot. Read on to discover the biggest, smallest, fastest, "toothiest," and more!

SHARKS

SIZE

LARGEST

The largest whale sharks can measure up to 40 feet long and weigh about 70,000 pounds.

LONGEST TAIL

The thresher shark's tail, at more than 12 feet, takes up more than half of the shark's overall body length.

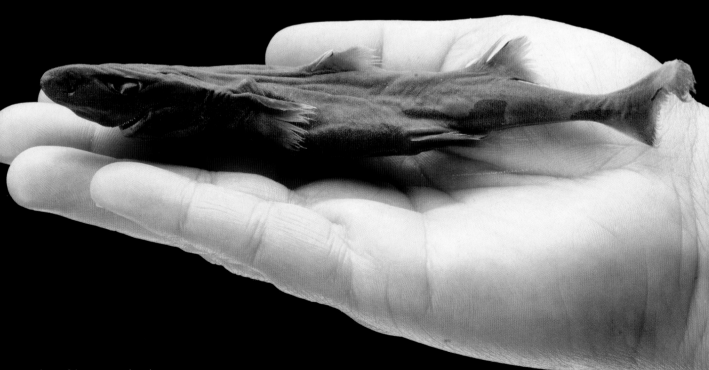

SMALLEST

Several types of dogfish shark have been measured at well under a foot long, fully grown. The spined pygmy shark reaches only 8 to 10 inches, and the dwarf lantern shark can be even tinier.

dwarf lantern shark

FASTEST

SHORTFIN MAKO

This speedy shark can rev it up to 40 miles per hour.

BLUE SHARK

Blue sharks can also swim close to 40 miles per hour. This speed is an asset during what is the longest shark migration—close to 1,200 miles in a season.

EXTREME SHARKS
TEETH

MOST TEETH

The whale, great white, and sand tiger sharks can have up to 3,000 teeth in their mouths over the course of their lives.

BIGGEST TOOTH

Some living sharks can have teeth up to three inches long. But none compares to the long-extinct megalodon, whose triangular teeth could measure more than seven inches, no wonder its name is Greek for "Big Tooth."

STRONGEST BITE

Chomp! The dusky shark's bite can exceed 130 pounds of force.

LIFE AND DEA

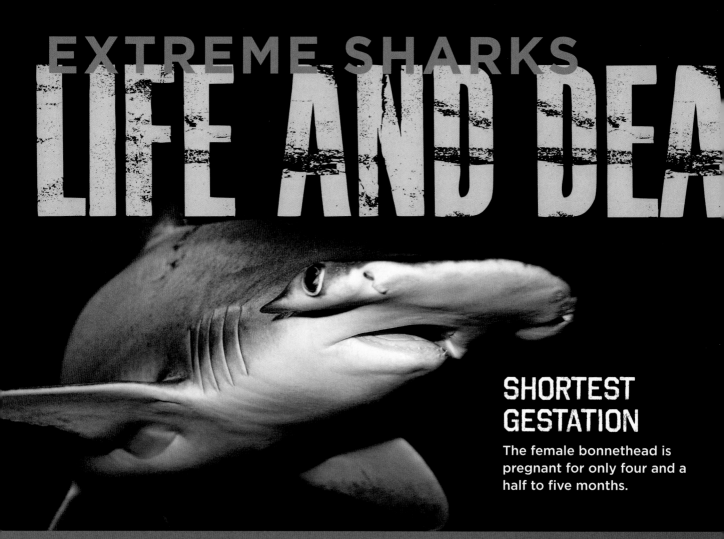

SHORTEST GESTATION

The female bonnethead is pregnant for only four and a half to five months.

LONGEST GESTATION

It's good the spiny dogfish has such a long lifespan. It also has the longest confirmed pregnancy, at 24 months. (The frilled shark *may* have a 42-month gestation period, but this is unconfirmed.)

LARGEST LITTER

The blue shark can give birth to up to 135 pups at a time. But a whale shark was found with more than 300 embryos inside.

LONGEST LIFESPAN

The spiny dogfish's estimated lifespan is about 75 years, though some experts say it can live for 100 years. Some scientists also believe the whale shark can reach the century mark.

MEGA SHA

Megalodon may not be around anymore. But there are still some enormous sharks out there, frightening prey wherever they go. Let's take a look at the world's biggest sharks!

Whale shark

One reason why they're called whale sharks is very clear: they are definitely as big as many whales. In fact, the whale shark is the world's largest living fish.

Those crazy spots and stripes might be an evolutionary connection to bottom-dwelling sharks, who often need camouflage. Another possibility is that sharks use the patterns to recognize and communicate with one another. Yet another reason might be as a sort of shield against ultraviolet radiation. Whatever the cause, that is one sharp-looking shark, with distinctive yellowish markings against its thick, dark gray skin.

Whale sharks also get their name from a feeding style similar to many whales: open wide and suck. These sharks are filter feeders, straining microscopic food particles from the water. And unlike other filtration-feeding creatures, the whale shark doesn't need to be moving forward to take in food. It has a unique suction system. When ready to eat, the whale shark often assumes a vertical position and feeds close to the surface. When the shark closes its mouth, the excess H_2O shoots back out through its gills.

Fitting for such a big shark, the whale shark has a particularly wide mouth. It is interestingly placed, as well: directly at the front of the head, instead of underneath like most sharks. Inside are 300 rows of teeth for each jaw. But the teeth are tiny and seem to play no role at all in the feeding process.

WH

Those aren't racing stripes: the whale shark has three ridges along each side of the body.

SHARK STATS

LENGTH **18–33 feet**

WEIGHT **40,000 lbs**

RANGE **Tropical waters**

ALE SHARK

SHARK BITE *A small car could fit into a whale shark's open mouth.*

GOING MY WAY?

Remora fish attach themselves to whale sharks by a suction-like process. The relationship between the two is described as commensalism: the remora gets transportation, protection, and food scraps; meanwhile, the shark doesn't really gain or lose anything. Due to this special friendship, the remora is also known by the charming name sharksucker.

CELEBRATING THE WHALE SHARK

Keep your White Houses and Lincoln Memorials. In the Philippines, the whale shark is featured on the back of the one-hundred-peso bill! The town of Donsol in the Philippines is considered the world's whale shark capital. The beautiful beasts are referred to locally as *butanding* and they are rightfully celebrated. There is an annual Butanding Festival with a parade and even a Ms. Butanding pageant. The great odds of seeing whale shark near Donsol—and swimming with them—has drawn an ever-increasing number of tourists to the town. This is potentially harmful for the sharks. As a result, the World Wildlife Fund established a strict set of guidelines for dealing with "butanding" safely, and regularly monitors the situation.

In Belize, whale sharks are known as Sapodilla Tom (referring to an area of common sightings). In Latin America, the distinctive pattern of light spots on a dark background has earned the shark the name *pez dama*—domino. In Kenya the name is *papa shilling.* Legend there has it that God was so pleased with the whale shark, he gave the angels gold and silver shilling coins to thrown down upon the shark. This is what gave the shark its spots. The names in Madagascar *(marokintana)* and Java *(geger lintang)* both refer to the spots as stars.

Whale sharks have been called gentle giants and can generally be considered harmless to humans. They're actually harmless to most creatures, except for plankton, small fish, and the occasional tuna or squid. They live in all the world's tropical and warm temperate waters, except for the Mediterranean. And the more plankton in the region, the better.

BASKING SH

The world's second-largest fish is the basking shark. So don't make fun of its nose. Even the scientific name, *Cetorhinus maximus,* comes from the Greek words for "marine monster," "nose," and "great."

The largest one ever recorded was 40 feet long. It was caught in herring nets in the Bay of Fundy in Canada in 1851. A report published the next year says, "The tail was seven feet nine inches in breadth...the head five feet across; the mouth three feet wide...."

The shark gets its name from a habit of feeding at the surface in warmer waters and seemingly "basking" in the sun's rays. They swim slowly near shore and are often spotted in pairs.

After its size and nose, you might notice its giant gills. Unlike other sharks, these go almost all the way around the head. The gills are very important in the basking shark's unique but passive feeding style. It is a filter feeder like the whale shark. But unlike the whale shark, the basking shark doesn't suck water in. It simply swims around with its mouth open. Gill rakers within the gills strain food from the water. These rakers can strain up to 2,000 tons of water an hour.

ARK

SHARK BITE *Sometimes basking sharks will join up in schools of 100 sharks or more.*

GREENLAND

SHARK STATS

LENGTH **21 feet**

WEIGHT **2,200 lbs**

RANGE **Deep seas, polar seas**

As the only shark daring enough to live in Greenland's chilly waters, it earned its location-specific name. The North Atlantic and Arctic is where this shark spends most of its time, though it's been spotted as far south as Antarctica. (Must like the cold.)

A massive shark, there have been reports of specimens measuring up to 24 feet long. It has a sluggish appearance and sluggish behavior to match. Though usually a solid gray, black, or brown, the shark's back and sides are sometimes marked with light spots or dark lines.

The Greenland shark's regular diet consists of herring, flounder, eel, and small sharks. Large groups of the sharks will gather near fisheries. However, this big shark likes big prey, and seals, porpoises, and even reindeer get eaten from time to time. It is also attracted to foul-smelling meat and will happily chow down on carrion when given the opportunity.

SHARK

SHARK BITE *There is a parasite,* Ommatokoita elongata, *that loves to attach itself to the Greenland's eye. This can impair the shark's vision or even cause blindness. The shark doesn't seem to mind too much, as it doesn't rely heavily on its very small eyes.*

SHARK SICKNESS

Fresh meat from a Greenland shark is poisonous. Dried meat, however, is edible. The meat, with its toxic chemical composition, is known to produce an intoxicating effect. As a result, when Greenland natives refer to a drunk person, they often use words that translate as "shark sick."

MEGA SHARKS
THRESHER

The thresher shark's caudal (tail) fin looks like something the Grim Reaper might carry around. This is a big shark, but that tail gives it half its length. The largest recorded thresher was nearly 25 feet long.

The bigeye thresher shark is very similar, though not quite as long: the maximum reported length is 16 feet. The bigeye also has fewer teeth: between 19 and 24 on the upper jaw, and 20 to 24 on the lower jaw. But what it lacks in length and teeth, it more than makes up for in eye size. The bigeye earned its name from its giant, oval, vertical eyes, which look up.

The thresher's diet is almost entirely bony fish, with the occasional squid mixed in. When feeding, they'll occasionally pair up or form a small group. They like to feed on schools of fish, and will slap at a school with their tails to stun the fish before eating them. The thresher shark is one of the breaching species that will leap partially or entirely out of the water. With those wicked tails, they've even been known to kill sea birds.

Generally a shy species, the thresher does not like to be approached. They are not aggressive and not a real threat to humans. They have been observed to attack boats, however.

SHARK STATS

LENGTH **20 feet**

WEIGHT **750–1,100 lbs**

RANGE **Oceanic and coastal waters**

SHARK

THRESHER TAIL TALES

People have been fascinated with thresher tails for a long, long time. From explorer Sir Richard Hawkins in 1622 comes a strange "tail tale" of a thresher shark who teamed up with a swordfish against a whale: "The Thresher is a greater fish, whose tayle is very broad & thick, and very waightie," Hawkins wrote. The thresher, "with its tayle thresheth upon the head of the Whale, till he force him to give way."

BLUNTNOSE SI

The bluntnose sixgill has a blunt nose and, on each side of its head, six gills. So you can probably guess how it got its name. And it's a "classic" look: the shark closely resembles fossilized images from 200 million years ago.

In an academic study from 2004, a bluntnose sixgill was officially measured at nearly 20 feet long. That is likely the largest recorded specimen of this species.

It's a lonely, mysterious life for the bluntnose sixgill. The shark seems to prefer solitude, and is only in the company of others to mate. It does not like to be touched, and will swim away from people. It spends the days resting on the sea floor. At night, the shark approaches the surface to feed. Prey include large bony fish (and nonbony ones too), shrimp, snails, crabs, and squid. If it finds some leftover bait, or a dead seal or sea lion, the bluntnose sixgill will not turn up its blunt nose.

Female bluntnose sixgills give birth to litters of anywhere from 22 to 108 shark pups.

SHARK STATS

LENGTH 16 feet

WEIGHT 1,500 lbs

RANGE Temperate and tropical waters

XGILL SHARK

SHARK BITE *From the structure of its mouth, it is guessed that the shark sneaks up on prey and catches it from the side.*

SHARK QUIZ

1. The prehistoric shark stethacanthus was unique because it...
A. didn't have claspers.
B. had an ironing board–shaped protrusion from its back.
C. is the one known predator of megalodon.

2. Breaching is the term used for...
A. adult sharks eating baby sharks of the same species.
B. annual migrations to warmer waters.
C. a shark's purposeful jump out of the water.

3. Sand tigers are the only shark species...
A. whose unborn embryos eat the fertilized and unfertilized eggs around them.
B. that gulp air from above the water's surface.
C. that are always born blind.

4. Which of these may be a sign of interest between male and female sharks?
A. Biting the females' fins
B. Male chasing the female
C. Female releasing pheromones
D. All of the above

5. With a filter feeder shark, what happens to the excess water that is swallowed?
A. It is shot out through the gills.
B. It is shot out through the blow hole.
C. It goes back out of the mouth.

6. Where are satellite tags attached to a shark?
A. On the pectoral (side) fin
B. On the dorsal (top) fin
C. They are wrapped in bait and swallowed.

7. The electroreceptors in sharks' heads are known as...
A. cladoselache.
B. the ampullae of Lorenzini.
C. remora.

8. What is the hammerhead shark's favorite meal?
A. Sea turtles
B. Squid
C. Stingrays

9. Which of the following sharks has been used as a "villain" in fiction, including Hemingway's *The Old Man and the Sea*?
A. Mako shark
B. Bull shark
C. Tiger shark

10. The novel and movie *Jaws* was inspired by a series of real-life shark attacks in...
A. Massachusetts.
B. Rhode Island.
C. New Jersey.